We R
PHON

Talent Night

TREASURE **BAY**

Parent's Introduction

Welcome to **We Read Phonics**! This series is designed to help you assist your child in reading. Each book includes a story, as well as some simple word games to play with your child. The games focus on the phonics skills and sight words your child will use in reading the story.

Here are some recommendations for using this book with your child:

1 Word Play

There are word games both before and after the story. Make these games fun and playful. If your child becomes bored or frustrated, play a different game or take a break.

I could make *thing* or *ring!*

Phonics is a method of sounding out words by blending together letter sounds. However, not all words can be "sounded out." **Sight words** are frequently used words that usually cannot be sounded out.

❷ Read the Story

After some word play, read the story aloud to your child—or read the story together, by reading aloud at the same time or by taking turns. As you and your child read, move your finger under the words.

Next, have your child read the entire story to you while you follow along with your finger under the words. If there is some difficulty with a word, either help your child to sound it out or wait about five seconds and then say the word.

❸ Discuss and Read Again

After reading the story, talk about it with your child. Ask questions like, "What happened in the story?" and "What was the best part?" It will be helpful for your child to read this story to you several times. Another great way for your child to practice is by reading the book to a younger sibling, a pet, or even a stuffed animal!

Would you like to take turns reading again, or would you like to read the whole story this time?

LEVEL 5 Level 5 introduces words with "ai" and "ay" with the long "a" sound (as in *bait* and *day*), "igh," "y," and "ie" with the long "i" sound (as in *high, cry,* and *tied*), and the "ng" sound (as in *song* and *king*). Also included are the word endings -er and -ing (as in *higher* and *running*).

Talent Night

A We Read Phonics™ Book
Level 5

Text Copyright © 2011 by Treasure Bay, Inc.
Illustrations Copyright © 2011 by Joe Kulka

Reading Consultants: Bruce Johnson, M.Ed., and Dorothy Taguchi, Ph.D.

We Read Phonics™ is a trademark of Treasure Bay, Inc.

Published by
Treasure Bay, Inc.
P.O. Box 119
Novato, CA 94948 USA

Printed in Singapore

Library of Congress Catalog Card Number: 2010932590

Hardcover ISBN: 978-1-60115-339-5
Paperback ISBN: 978-1-60115-340-1

We Read Phonics™
Patent Pending

Visit us online at:
www.TreasureBayBooks.com

PR-11-10

Talent Night

By Paul Orshoski

Illustrated by Joe Kulka

Alphabet Soup

Creating words using certain letter combinations will help your child read this story.

Materials: thick paper or cardboard; scissors; pencils, crayons, or markers; small cooking pot and stirring spoon

1. Cut 23 two x two inch squares from the paper or cardboard and print these letters and letter combinations on the squares: ai, igh, y, ight, ang, ing, ong, ung, f, t, p, r, d, ch, g, n, l, b, s, h, sh, th, and k.

2. Place the letters into a pretend pot of soup.

3. Players stir the letters. Each player takes a letter from the pot. Stir again. Each player takes another letter. When a player can make a word by putting his letters together, he makes the word and reads it out loud.

4. Continue stirring. Each player continues to take additional letters and make words.

   The player with the most words at the end wins.

Words that can be made with these letters include *tail, pail , gain, high, night, right, lights, bright, sight, shy, things, spring, rang, hung, song,* and *king.*

Word Cubes

This is a fun way to practice some sight words used in the story.

Materials: paper or thin cardboard, pencil, scissors, tape

1. Using the pattern in the illustration, make two cube outlines on a separate piece of paper or thin cardboard.

2. Before cutting out or folding, write each of the following 12 words, on one face of each of the two cube outlines:

   laugh, little, some, saw, very, they, show, won, walk, play, was, into

3. Cut out the cube outline. Fold on the dotted lines. Tape the flaps to make the two cubes.

4. Now roll the cubes. Read out loud the two words shown on top.

5. Try to make up a sentence that uses both of the words.

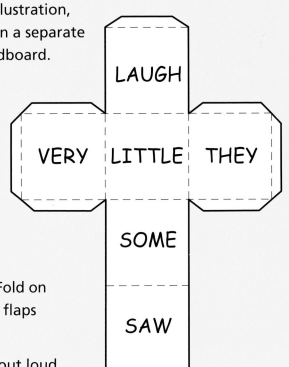

I came on stage for Talent Night.

I had them laughing left and right.

The lights were bright
and right on me.

I did some things you had to see.

I cracked a joke and spun a tale.
I sang a song and rode a snail.

And then I did a thing way neat.
I played a flute with my two feet.

I sprung a tiger from my hat.

I did a hand-spring on a mat.

I hung a king snake by the tail.

I dove into a little pail.

And then I flung a set of eggs
while standing up on just one leg.

My act, it was a real big hit.
To end, I chose shy Pam to sit.

I had her spin a lemon pie.

I made her vanish in the sky.

Then when she came back in sight,
I saw her hanging from a light.

She fell onto a swinging bar.
It swung her high and very far.

On a wire she did land. She walked
the line while on her hands.

She hung on tight, and then she fell.

But I must say she landed well.

By then shy Pam was all the rage.
They sent her up to center stage.

I got the pie right in my face.

But Pam was glad. She won first place.

I am thinking of a word that starts with the "mmm" sound.

I Am Thinking

Blending letter sounds together helps children read new words.

1 Think of a person, place, or thing from the book.

2 Say, "I am thinking of a word from the book that starts with a 'k' sound (make the sound of the letter 'k'), and ends with the 'ing' sound (make the sound of 'ing' as in *sing*). What is the word?" The answer is *king.*

3 Use a variety of different words from the story. Present the first part of the word and then the second part of the word. It could be the first sound and then the rest of the word, or it could be the first syllable and then the second syllable.

4 Continue with additional words from the story. For variation, ask your child to take a turn and ask you to guess the word.

Appropriate words from the story include *bright, things, spring, hanging, swinging, center, laughing, standing, pail, vanish,* and *song.*

Phonics Game

Codes

Playing with letters is a wonderful way to reinforce letters and sounds.

1 On a sheet of paper, write these words in code:

mhfgs, kztfg, szkdms, kdes, qhfgs, shfdq, rmzjd, rszfd

2 Your child can "break the code" by rewriting the words using the next letter in the alphabet. For example, the letter "d" becomes the letter "e." The letter "z" is used for the letter "a." If necessary, copy the alphabet on the top of the paper.

3 Answers are: *night, laugh, talent, left, right, tiger, snake, stage*

4 For more word play, try to write a sentence from the story in code, changing each letter to the next letter in the alphabet.

If you liked *Talent Night,*
here is another **We Read Phonics** book you are sure to enjoy!

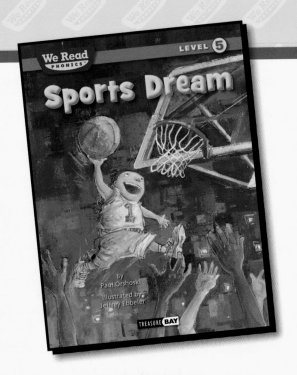

Sports Dream

A boy dreams of being a great sports star. In his dreams he is the best player in every sport: basketball, baseball, soccer, hockey, dirt bike races, and even fishing! However, he is really only great at one thing in sports—he is a great sports fan!